Byron

you are a star!

BE AMAZING,

Surthrival

MODE

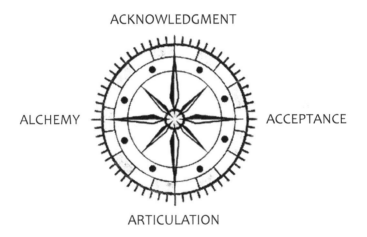

ACKNOWLEDGMENT

ALCHEMY

ACCEPTANCE

ARTICULATION

BY
PERVIS TAYLOR, III, M.A.

This book is dedicated to every man who's struggled...

Acknowledgments

Jesus. My parents Pervis (R.I.P.) and Jacquelyn. My siblings Jocelyn, Jerrod, and Tajare. My nephews: Gavin and Paxton; and niece, Ellie. To the host of loving, supportive friends (too many to name) thank you for everything! Shout to The Black Whole! My Aunt Jackie, Uncle James, and Dr. AR. Bernard for always assuring me of God's love and presence. Lastly, thank you to the city of Lancaster, Texas for helping me redefine what it means to be human, masculine, and gifted.
Be Great!!

Table of Contents

Sur-thrive-al

MODE

"Surthrive" means to triumph over and transmute the narrative of a debilitating situation from victimization to one of power and strength.

Introduction

Hello brothers! I hope this book finds you well. Thanks for picking this up. Whether you got it from your wife, your girl, a friend, or if the subject matter just interests you, this book is for you. I pray that the words on these pages cause you to think, reflect, ponder, and act. Enjoy!!

This book is all about surviving AND thriving. In life, many of us go through situations that we must overcome. Being a survivor is only the beginning. I know many of us wear survival of past situations, ordeals, and the like as badges of honor. After all, there is the natural feeling to want to celebrate after having come through a terrible situation still in one piece. You have the Destiny's Child song "Survivor" and the television show of the same name. Also, there are support groups for people who have survived cancer, rape, or natural disasters. Surviving something is a very powerful thing. However, there's a step beyond that which is key to truly overcoming, and that is thriving. I decided to build a bridge in the form of creating a hybrid between survival and thriving and came up with "surthrival." I say in my book *Pervis Principles Volume 2* that "life was designed for you to thrive, not just survive." This revelation came to me many years ago while in deep introspection. See, for me in particular, I found that in my life's narrative, I needed to go beyond just surviving the trauma I experienced; I needed to crush it beneath my feet. I've experienced it all: molestation, emasculation, low self-esteem, bullying, identity crisis, toxic masculinity, and depression—and this is all before the age of eighteen. From there the aforementioned intensified when I had to deal with poverty, betrayal, spiritual darkness, homelessness, and rejection. I wasn't content in just barely making it out of my struggles. There had to be another side to this. They say that curiosity killed the cat. However, for me curiosity brought me to a place of self-actualization in thriving. I'll share and unpack that curiosity in this book.

Blocks to Change and Transformation

In medicine, there's a term called FTT, which means "failure to thrive." The term is used in pediatrics and for veterans who experience severe weight loss and fail to catch up to their peers. Notice the abbreviation isn't FTS, "failure to survive." Even in medicine, doctors and professionals are looking for a person to thrive.

I believe the greatest lie we ingest is that we can't change or transform. Change and transformation seem almost philosophical, especially in the age of social media. We as a culture have become accustomed to looking the part but not being the part. We pretend to be champions, yet inside we still are victims. Why? Firstly, it's easy and comforting. Secondly, many of us romanticize the pain and trauma that we've experienced, and rarely do we truly triumph over it. Lastly, we don't typically see transformation modeled in our lives, especially in our families. People think to their level of exposure. It's my hope that if I expose you to the truth that things can change for the better.

From Hurting to Surthriving

I love all of my clients. They range from celebrities to executives to youths. However, young men hold a special place in my heart. My most audacious goal is to give them the tools that I hadn't received when I was their age. Moreover, I want to equip them to become 21st century "surthrivalists" so they are as whole as they can be. Many of our young men are hurting and have been victimized—not only interpersonally but also culturally. Young men of color, in particular, are not allowed or given permission to just be human.

They don't know how to process. No matter the socioeconomic background, I've found this to be true across the board. Young men are inundated with messaging about what it means to be masculine daily. The same is true for adult men. Yet there is very few messaging about how to heal from their wounds or pain.

The problem with this is that an emotionally challenged man was once an emotionally challenged boy. I recall a few years back being hired by a youth organization in Washington, D.C. They wanted me to coach their leadership staff in their youth development program. The leaders were split into groups by gender. I had the young men first. I wanted to engage the men in emotional intelligence and processing. I must add that these were young men from the community. So many of them had been in gangs, sold drugs, and just experienced many hardships. As always at the beginning of all my sessions, I tell my story as transparently as I can. I do this to create a level playing field. Yes, I'm the "expert," but I'm also a human being. Truth and vulnerability can be so disarming. After I told my story, one young man raised his hand and wanted to share. He shared how he, being thirty years old at the time, had never mourned or grieved his mother's death when he was five years old. That young man cried his eyes out. What I witnessed wasn't a thirty-year-old man. I witnessed a five-year-old boy crying. Another young man shared how in twisting his knee he missed out on the opportunity of a lifetime: a full scholarship to a major university. He was overcome with emotion. In that moment, I realized how victimized men can be. These men might have survived the traumas (barely). But they hadn't transmuted the narratives of their lives. They hadn't stepped on the other side of the pain with power and victory.

I've encountered so many young men and adult men alike who are just at the stage of survival or, much worse, suppression of their pain. Many of them are hugely successful. One of the great deceptions is the belief that just because a person is successful or seemingly achieving great things in life that they have sur-thrived. Not true. Many "successful" people have many areas of their lives where they aren't thriving; they're just surviving.

I look at #metoo movement. It's a perfect example of surthriving. Collectively, the once victims of sexual misconduct and assault are now empowered vessels of change. The narrative has been transmuted and turned into something more powerful than before.

I look at individuals like Viktor Frankl, acclaimed psychologist who learned how to thrive after being subjected to cruelty and mistreatment after spending years in a concentration camp. He later developed a psychological approach, logo therapy. I look at Ishmael Beah, a former child solider from Sierra Leone who was brainwashed and killed hundreds of people while being addicted to drugs and who today is an inspirational speaker and best-selling author. There are many more examples of surthrival I could share, but the point I want to stress is that surthriving is possible! I say to my clients and mentees all the time: No one is born ill-equipped, they're just born ill-informed. That means that every man has within himself the capacity to triumph over adversity, whether it be physical, emotional, mental, or spiritual. Not only to triumph but to transmute the narrative of said adversity to something of power. The challenge has been that no one has informed them! My goal is that this book serves notice to men from all walks of life that they can overcome and trample under their feet the pains they've experienced.

I don't desire to engage in a battle of the sexes. Let's face it, there are a plethora of books on how to do this and how to do that. By large, many self-help, spiritual, or personal development books are read by women. It's a fact of life that women are more likely to engage in a process of sustainable transformation quicker than men. Additionally, a lot of women aren't afraid of confronting emotional trauma or adversity. Women also, for the most part, are actualized in numerous ways. They are friends, mothers, lovers, daughters, sisters, creators, and much more. Conversely, for men, there's a cultural norm of toxic masculinity whereby a man's masculinity is measured by his sexual conquests, achievements, salary, and his ability to exercise Alpha-like traits. Men, especially men of color, aren't given space or permission to be human let alone process the experiences of life. A man is only actualized in his output and outcomes. Men and manhood are in a crisis. However, I believe crisis births opportunity. This is an opportune time to have the difficult conversation. Moreover, it's time to really face head on the lies we've believed as it relates to masculinity and emotions. Here's the truth: it is possible to surthrive in life. I know because I've done it. As a coach and mentor, I've shared with ALL my clients and mentees that I'd never advise something that I myself haven't done or wouldn't do.

I know that for many of us men, we probably won't seek out a therapist. I've learned that you have to meet people where they are. For some, this will be it! What I want to provide is something relatively simple (through practice) that you can put in your healthy emotional toolbox.

I've come up with what I call the 4A's of surthrival mode: Acknowledgment, Acceptance, Articulation, and Alchemy.

All I ask is that you just believe that it's possible for you to overcome, to experience wholeness, to have peace within your emotions, and rest from anxiety. IT IS POSSIBLE. One thing that it is important to note: I did see a therapist. I believe that therapy is essential to the process of healing. However, what I'm offering and proposing are DIY (do it yourself) tips that my clients and I personally used and currently use to get through and finally to sur-thrive!!!

Before you turn the page and begin, I want to establish some tenets for surthriving. We have the four modes, but there are some rules that we must abide by if we are to surthrive. They'll be mentioned in various forms throughout the book. However, I think it's important that we establish these rules early on!

*We and we alone are responsible for our mental and emotional health.

*Confronting our mental and emotional health is very masculine.

*The power of a secret is in keeping it. (There's nothing new under the sun.)

*Emotional health is mental health.

*We must be intentional about improving our mental and emotional lives.

*Everything is a process. (No shortcuts!)

SURTHRIVAL MODE

Surthrival Mode 1
ACKNOWLEDGMENT

"But sometimes pain had to be acknowledged and even touched so that one could move into it and through it and past it. Or else be destroyed by it."

— Mary Balogh

I often joke that we as a society are in the poker face era. We want to look cool, calm, and together. We want to look as though we've never experienced anything bad or that nothing has ever hurt us. I used to try to be like this. But I had a problem. The pain I kept experiencing was so present and so powerful in my being that I could hardly breathe or move. I used to say to myself, Man this hurts like hell; I'm not too good at pretending. I remember being twenty-eight years old and going through probably one of the hardest times of my life. My dad had died suddenly a few years earlier. I was feeling down about my career, I had severe loneliness, I hated where I lived, and I was extremely depressed and felt purposeless. I was in such a dark place that I'd stay in my apartment for days on end and not leave.

Interestingly enough, that time in my life had more to do with my earlier life. I found myself thinking about all the painful experiences I had as a child. Whenever I found myself in my depression, all I could think about was my childhood. To be honest, I had blocked out a majority of my childhood in my mind. I was so focused on trying to be successful and famous that I hid myself from myself. One night, I couldn't take it anymore. I was gonna do something crazy or I was going to get through this. I remember lying prostrate on the floor crying out to God for help. I lay there for hours. When I picked myself up, I went to my Bible, and this one scripture (James 5:16; NIV) popped out to me: "Therefore confess your sins to each other and pray for each other so that you may be healed." At the time, I didn't connect it as I do today, but I just literally took that scripture and I did my best to apply it. I ended up doing something I'd never witnessed another man do: acknowledge his hurt and pain. I remember calling a friend and just literally having diarrhea of the mouth, so to speak. I acknowledged that I had anger with my dad and his perception of me and my masculinity and sexuality. I acknowledged that at the age of seven I was molested by a friend. I acknowledged that I always felt inadequate as a man, largely in part due to the fact that I was emasculated daily during my high school years. As I went down the list, unburdening myself, I realized that I was starting to feel lighter. Depression can affect you physically. For me, I experienced lethargy and heaviness daily. After that conversation with my friend, I literally in that moment felt lighter.

I want you to imagine for a second. Imagine that the worst pain you've felt suddenly just subsided. The crazy thing about it is that we've become so accustomed to living a certain way that we've acclimatized ourselves to dysfunction. In other words, we've taken on abnormality as a normality. Now, I believe in being balanced, and I don't recommend spouting off at the mouth like I did. However, what I'm saying is that there's a power in acknowledgment of an issue outside of yourself. This takes courage. I've noticed that in life there's a connection between acknowledgment and courage. I always believe that under every action there's a supportive and/or congruent emotion or feeling to undergird it. Like a person lashing out in anger, underneath that is usually the feeling of being hurt. So whenever I acknowledge something, I'm always reminded of the courage it took to do so. Being courageous is one of the most powerful things to be, especially as it relates to pain and adversity. All too often, rather than acknowledge or confess a truth, we bury it or pretend it's not there.

The problem is when we bury the truth, we have to do the painstaking work of digging it up. Let me caution you: it's not only painstaking, but it will cost you more than you realize. One of the young men I mentor tried to commit suicide. I'm sharing this to express the gravity and importance of why we need to exhibit courage early on and acknowledge the things that are not working in our lives sooner rather than later. I always make myself available to my mentees, and I do my best to instill in them as well as this life principle of *only what you acknowledge and confess can be healed* (derived from James 5:16). So this particular mentee decided that he was going to end his life by jumping off a bridge. Thankfully, he decided at the last minute to call the police. He ended up spending a week in a psychiatric hospital. That was in itself a traumatic experience. Having to take meds, repeating himself over and over again to strangers who he sensed weren't invested in him, and having to face his frantic mother was a heavy weight to bear. When we spoke, he said to me, "Pervis, I let this feeling of depression get to a place of almost ending my life. I could've prevented this pain if I just would've told you or someone close that I was hurting this deeply." He went on to share with me that he knew I was available but he just couldn't muster up the courage to admit that he was hurting.

MODE 1: ACKNOWLEDGMENT

Whenever I work with my clients, one of the first places I try to access and appeal to is their sense of courage and bravery. Why? Because I know that if I can access that place, I know that at some point the acknowledgment of the real issues will come to the surface. That's the important thing to note: the real issues. For men, we often don't truly know the real issues that need to be acknowledged. However, we do know that there is deep underpinning of hurt that we experience. I recently worked with a group of young men in Brooklyn. My business partner and I have made great strides to build a rapport with these young men. One thing I know for sure is that when you do get a man to a place where he's comfortable to acknowledge something you have a small window of opportunity for truth. So this particular day, we had them in a place of comfort. I asked them as sincerely as I could how many of them suffered from anxiety. Every hand went up in the room. I followed up with praise for their bravery and honesty in sharing. Once my partner and I kept accessing that place of courage, they continued to share deeper issues. Now every issue wasn't resolved in our session. But, what happened was there was a noticeable shift in the atmosphere. Why? Because there was a lifting of burdens off of these young men. Acknowledgment is a powerful tool that's underused in today's climate.

When you unpack and explore the concept of acknowledgment further, you'll find that it's tied to shame and negativity. Think about any family. There are secrets within that family that everyone knows about, but they know never to speak of them. While I understand to a degree the concept of not bringing up dirt for "protection" reasons of particular family members, I know now that it's so destructive. We know that a child has been molested, yet we don't speak on it. Meanwhile, that young boy or girl is headed for a life of severe pain. Yet, we choose silence over acknowledging the dysfunction. Essentially, our families are teaching us shame and secrecy are a way of life. Moreover, that silence gives consent. So many people, especially men, are walking around with a sense of shame. Shame over not achieving, shame over their relationships, shame over sexual encounters (or lack of), shame over abuse, shame over molestation, and shame over an unfulfilled life. Believe it or not, there are more men who have or are currently experiencing this level of shame. To take it a step further, many of them do not know that they're experiencing shame. The cycle of dysfunction continues on until one person is brave enough to break it. However, there is usually a penalty attached to that act of bravery. We see it in the news. If a person acknowledges that they were raped or mistreated, their character comes into question. They get called names and social media all of a sudden becomes a divided war zone. All over acknowledgment of a thing. We are in a culture of secrecy and deception. The greatest threat to a person's true healing will always be the culture. Acknowledgment is countercultural. Being emotionally healthy is countercultural!

I remember when Tyler Perry was on Oprah and he was sharing his story of being molested as a child. The entire audience was filled with men (a first for her show). All the men had one thing in common: they too were molested. Watching the show was a powerful experience for me to witness so many men go against the cultural norm of secrecy. So many men were set free from that one episode. Granted freedom and healing are a process; they began the journey that day. From that one episode thousands of men all over the world got help that day. In those men getting healed, guess what? Everything attached to them got healed as well. Their relationships with others and themselves got mended, all from acknowledging the truth.

I remember being asked to speak on a panel in Baltimore. The topic was ask-men-so-women-can-be-more-informed type of thing. What was so powerful about the experience was that the other men that were on the panel with me were very honest and truthful about their life experiences. As I stated earlier, when you level the playing field with honesty, it creates an atmosphere for honesty, sharing, and acknowledgment. One woman asked me a question: "Why is it that I'm hurting so bad after my divorce and my ex-husband just seemingly moved on and remarried?" She was visibly hurt and still grieving over the loss of her marriage. I replied to her, "The fact that you are able to acknowledge that you're still hurting and grieving, believe it or not, you're doing better than him. By the time you've gone through the process, you're going to be able to be healthy for your next relationship. Meanwhile, he's going to eventually implode." I remember my old Bible study teacher Chris Burge said a statement that never left me: men scream at a frequency that only they can hear. It's true. Even though it looks like her ex-husband has moved on, he's going to suffer in the end. **Because whatever we refuse to acknowledge masters and rules us, period.** Acknowledgment is the gateway to healing that is possible for us.

I often study various programs for development or recovery to see what modalities they use as part of their processes. One thing I've noticed in my research is that all programs incorporate acknowledgment into their curriculum. AA (Alcoholics Anonymous) is one of the top mutual aid organizations in the world. They have a high success rate for various reasons. However, I wanted to highlight that one of AA's tenants that it emphasizes over and over again is that at every meeting each participant acknowledges that he or she is an alcoholic. I know on the surface it may seem a bit redundant or excessive, but actually what's happening is that every time a person confesses, the person is actually loosening the grip of shame and guilt and is simultaneously reclaiming his or her power.

So far in this chapter, I've shared the concept of acknowledgment as it relates to sharing some painful things, the bravery and courage that come along with that, in addition to the consequences of not acknowledging things. However, I would like to offer that, with almost everything, there's a spectrum. Acknowledgment is no exception. While there's power in confessing a truth, there's also power in acknowledgment of the great things we have going on within ourselves. Plus, I wouldn't be a good life coach if I didn't incorporate this (smile).

There's a wonderful organization called Black Men Smile. The purpose of the organization is to break the narrative that black men do not smile. Being from the hyper-masculine south, I thought this was true. In every picture with my friends or family, no men or boys smiled in the pics. I liked to smile, but of course I wanted to fit in. So I joined the club and stopped smiling. Until one day one day while I was in undergrad working on a group project, my friend Melissa said to me, "Pervis you have a beautiful smile." That moment changed my entire life. Up until that point I couldn't think of anything that I had that was worthy to be acknowledged in a positive sense. I was underweight, short, had acne and severe eczema. I suffered from extremely low self-esteem. However, when she said that to me, I believed her. I found something about myself physically that I could acknowledge that I liked. You know what the end result was? By finding that one thing that I truly could embrace helped me to build the foundation to a self-appreciation that hadn't existed before. As dramatic as that may sound, it's the truth.

As I stated before, when we confess a thing we can bring healing. I would like to add that what we confess and acknowledge also brings power. I've learned along my journey that you may not always be confident, but if you always have power you're going to be okay.

MODE 1: ACKNOWLEDGMENT

When I work with my clients I don't approach it as a "one size fits all" type of thing. That's because as people we are not monolithic. We come in various shapes and sizes and have various backstories that contribute to our unique makeups. However, whenever I have a male client, in our first session, I always ask him to name (acknowledge) three things that make him wonderful. So far, I have yet to encounter a male as a client who's able to do so initially. Even the "successful" clients have trouble doing so. If they are able to name something it's usually related to their success. The reason why I do this more extensively with my male clients is because I know that if I experienced lack of worthiness for much of my life, then other men too must've felt the same way. Now I'm not generalizing all men. What I am saying, though, is that men do tend to have issues when it comes to acknowledging the positive within themselves. Everyone does. But it doesn't get talked about enough with men. Again, there's a culture that says that men don't have issues with certain things, only women do. I'll give you an example. One of my clients is an amazingly talented filmmaker and actor. He's worked on television shows and movies. He's a tall, handsome man who definitely stands out in the room. However, he had much trouble finding and accessing the great things within himself. He didn't have problems acknowledging the negative though, and he was very keen on what was wrong in his life. One day, he sends me a headshot. I was floored when I saw it. In this picture, my client—who can be very demure and almost invisible—was so pronounced, poised, and commanding. No wonder he booked roles. This dude has it! I was confused because who I sat with weekly wasn't the guy in the pic. I remember holding the pic up to him, and I said, "Can you say something positive about this guy." He couldn't. However, I could name at least five remarkable things about him. What I learned from that client and even from my own narrative is the importance of daily positive acknowledgments. This positive reinforcement practice can begin to shift and alter the very structure of our brains. Neuroplasticity is the building of a new neural pathway in the brain. This process is a key factor into engaging in surthriving versus just getting by. So as men we need to actively participate in this practice every day.

What happens more often than not in men, especially, is we don't acknowledge that we overcompensate and present ourselves as cocky. Now there are some men out there who are not shy about owning who they are and rare instances can back it up. However, in a lot of cases those men are really just protecting themselves from being exposed as insecure. Acknowledgment of the positive is rooted in power whereas overcompensation or cockiness can tend to be rooted in confidence. Yes you read correctly. I said confidence. Now one might ask is confidence a bad thing. Absolutely not! However, the difference between power and confidence is this: confidence is having an assuredness that one can do a task well. Power, on the other hand, means that regardless of if one can do it well or not, they still possess greatness and value. **Men, it's time we start to acknowledge who we are as just human beings.** We have wonderful things about us that have nothing to do with what we do or achieve. OK. So let's put this into practice. Right now, take a few moments to reflect. Acknowledge five things about yourself. I'll go first: I'm a great friend, I'm honest, I'm dependable, I'm consistent, and I'm fun. To be honest, I can acknowledge some more great things about myself. I just wanted to give you a realistic look at how you see yourselves. If it was easy for you to do, great. If it was a challenge, do your best to find something. I know it's there. Do this practice daily. Preferably in the morning in the mirror.

I know what I'm introducing may be novel to us as men, but one thing is for certain: this is a key component to the emotional and mental wellness we all desire (whether we admit it or not). As with everything in life, this requires consistency and time. It is a process. I implore you to commit to do this (on both sides: pain and power). Eventually, it will become a habit and second nature. This will lead to getting through situations quicker, expand us, and deepen our capacity for fulfillment and enjoyment.

Surthrival Mode 2
ACCEPTANCE

"The first step toward change is awareness.
The second step is acceptance."
— Nathaniel Branden

I remember I took a class on conflict resolution. At the time, I thought I knew all the components to resolving a conflict like the back of my hand. My professor made a statement that shocked me. She said, "What are you willing to accept in a conflict?" I thought long and hard at how absurd that sounded. What did I need to accept? More than likely they were wrong. Hence, why there is a conflict! Then as she unpacked it further, it all made sense. Acceptance is not to be mistaken as condoning something. It means to accept that it happened; nothing more nothing less. For example, some of us have to accept the fact that our fathers weren't in our lives. We're not condoning it, we're just accepting that it's true. One of the hardest things you'll ever have to do is accept something, especially if it's something we don't desire or is painful. That particular class revolutionized my thinking as it relates to not only conflict but for life as a whole. It changed my approach to coaching. It shifted a lot of things for me. I believe that this stage is the secret sauce or secret weapon that many will overlook because of the simplicity of it.

I remember leaving that class and as I was walking to my destination I began to get reflective about my life. My life has never been what most would consider normal. As a man, I often found myself in flux because I wanted to just fit in and be like everyone else. I desired it so badly that I remember asking God to take away my gifting as a coach and mentor in an exchange for a normal life. That was one of the first things I had to accept. My life was just different. I had to accept the fact that I didn't have all the wild sexual escapades my friends or cousins had. I had to accept that I didn't have a date to the prom. I had to accept that I was at odds with myself. I had to accept the fact that many women won't get me because my brand of masculinity looks different than most men. I had to accept betrayal from someone who I thought was my brother and best friend. I had to accept that at my age my life didn't turn out the way I envisioned—including not having a family as of yet and still plowing my way through entrepreneurship and the struggles that come with it. I had to accept the fact that in spite of the positive picture I paint and have painted of my dad, that he was a drug user and did a lot of damage to his family. I could go on and on about things I accepted. Needless to say, I felt a freedom that I never experienced before. What acceptance brought for me was a sense of clarity. It enabled me to see so many perspectives that I didn't see before. Moreover, it laid out a clear path for me. It allowed me to have empathy not only for myself but also for others involved in my situations. For example, in the class we had to find an unresolved conflict in our lives. It didn't have to be dire but just unresolved. I chose what I feel to be my family's lack of support for me. I remember being the first grandchild to graduate from college. There was no celebration. When I wrote my first book, my family didn't support me by buying books. When I was featured in my first magazine article, my family didn't call to congratulate me. Lastly, when I was on television they didn't call to say how proud they were of me. My dad was my biggest cheerleader. I never noticed my family's lack of support until he passed.

Difference between Acknowledgment and Acceptance

I know you may be thinking that these two are similar and can often be used interchangeably. And you would be right in a regular circumstance. However, as it relates to the processing of issues and emotions, they are two different things. If you can imagine, acknowledgment is like getting your high school diploma. While acceptance is getting your Ph.D. Acknowledgment is the recognition of a thing. Acceptance is not only recognizing a thing but also being responsible for that thing and how it has affected your life. Acceptance carries a lot more weight. In fact, in the process of grieving, the last stage of that process is called acceptance. Like survival is good, but thriving is the optimal. The same applies to acknowledgment vs. acceptance.

What did I have to accept in the above scenario? First, I had to accept my position in the conflict. I had to accept that I wanted recognition for my hard work. I then had to accept that my family isn't that celebratory in general. Next, I had to accept that my father, although imperfect, was my biggest cheerleader and he was no longer here. I had to accept that in spite of my perceived lack of support, that my family loved me. There were many other things that I just had to accept about this conflict. What that acceptance led to was empathy for my family. I was able to put myself in my family's shoes. My mother is a brilliant woman and at one time a talented dancer. I remember one time she admitted to me that she admired my audaciousness to follow my dreams. It made me think about what she gave up to become a wife and mother. As for my sister, she at the time hadn't reached her potential as the amazing woman she is. She was trying to figure out her life and navigate through her own trauma. My little brother is married and has two kids, one who was on the spectrum. He too, at the time, hadn't realized his brilliance as an academic. Once I was able to put myself in their shoes, it provided clarity and more understanding as to how they perceive and walk through life. **So ultimately, what acceptance did was that it didn't change the situation; it changed me.**

A graver scenario to highlight is the life of Viktor Frankl. Frankl was a highly noted psychiatrist known for his unique approach to psychology. He wrote a book entitled *Man's Search for Meaning*. The book is a visceral and poignant first-person perspective take at life in the concentration camp as a Jewish person during the Holocaust. Moreover, it graphically depicts the cruelty that was unjustly inflicted upon the people. From starvation to beatings and more beatings and for some the gas chamber, the book vividly captures the rawness of the marrow of hate that humans unfortunately have the capacity to exhibit. Rather than resist or delude himself, Frankl chose to accept the reality of his situation. It was a transformational moment in his life. What he found after his acceptance was his belief that if a person can accept where they are and understand that they have a purpose in life that they must fulfill, they can endure anything. The acceptance enabled him to live through the torment. He endured hunger, seeing his friends wither away, verbal and mental abuse, and severe isolation. Frankl's acceptance was two-fold. He accepted that for this part of his life he was in a concentration camp. He also accepted that he had a purpose, something greater than himself that was to be expressed by him and him alone. What a revelation! His story is an excellent example of surthriving. He later would develop a new therapeutic approach called logo therapy, which proposes that if a person can accept that there's more for them, they will be able to persevere through anything in life to get to their promised place.

Surrender

I often think about Frankl's account when I'm in an introspective place in my life. One aspect or component of acceptance that I feel isn't talked about is surrender. The word surrender is often looked at from a place of weakness or powerlessness. However, there is great strength and power in surrendering. I think about Jesus when he saw before him that he was to be crucified that he uttered the words, "Father, if you are willing, take this cup from me; yet not my will, yours be done" (Luke 22:42; NIV). Jesus, in an honest moment, reconsidered what his mission was to be. However, he surrendered and accepted the fact that though what he was to endure would be humiliating and painful, he knew that a greater purpose and significance lay ahead. There's a power that comes with acceptance. It will break you through to a new level. But it's not easy to choose. Like acknowledgment, acceptance is only for the brave. Those willing to let go of the protective mechanisms they developed to shield them from life will begin to see and experience life in a new way. Acceptance can save your life. Surrendering can save your life. Everything in life is a process. I believe that we're either going into a process or coming out of a process. The goal? Either to make you whole or keep you broken. With acceptance, one can begin to go along the process of healing. I liken it to working out with a trainer after you haven't worked out in a while. You first have to accept that you aren't in shape. Then you have to accept that probably the next day you're going to be sore. Finally, you must accept the fact that if you continue the workout plan, you will see results.

I touched on this earlier with the things I had to accept. But I want to reiterate acceptance of things as they are, not as we desire, yields many benefits. But I think for many of us it's hard to do so. Acceptance can almost feel like defeat or cowering out of the situation. The way to accept a thing is that we first must rebrand our relationship with our perception of acceptance. Acceptance is not powerlessness; in fact, it is powerful. Acceptance isn't cowardly; in fact, it is quite bold. Acceptance isn't weakening; it's in fact healing and restorative. One of the biggest benefits of acceptance is that it helps us with our expectations. Underneath our hurts, disappointments, and frustrations lie the biggest culprit of our pain: expectations. We hurt because we had an expectation of something or someone. More often than not, that expectation usually is underwhelming and not met. We tend to think in terms of ideals. Things should be this way or things should go that way. While there is truth in those thoughts, let's face it. Life usually doesn't go the way we plan. What acceptance of a situation does is it mitigates the pain and disappointment attached to our expectation of the situation. All too often we walk around with pain that we don't know what to do with. And for many of us men, we don't know where it came from. So to circumvent this, we must grow to a place where we have to embrace the realities of our lives. Once we do so, we learn to manage our expectations in the process. As a person who's worked for themselves for nearly a decade, this was a tough but needed lesson. I can't tell you how many times I've had folks interested in my services even go so far as to book an appointment and at the last millisecond, cancel. So what was my expectation in all of this? I expect people to be people. What does that mean? I know there are some committed folks, some uncommitted folks, and everything in between. In managing this expectation with acceptance, I now recover quickly when I encounter a flaky person. To be honest, I'm not typically good at recovery in these circumstances. However, in learning to manage my expectations, I'm much better. What is true for me, is true for you.

Delusion

Switching gears for a moment. I would like to talk about that enormous elephant in the room that I've noticed amongst people, but especially in men. Delusion.

When we are afraid to deal or ACKNOWLEDGE a thing, we tend to create an alternate universe called delusion. If we can't acknowledge a thing, we certainly can't accept a thing. I've worked with far too many people who are willing to be delusional. They have gone to great lengths to play pretend with their lives. I know one man who refused to accept that he was molested. He always addressed the issue as he was just experimenting. I would often ask, "How were you experimenting and you were five and the person was an adult?" He stuck to his guns and seemingly went on with life unscathed, or so it seemed. We lost touch with each other, but I would check in on him via social media. Everything looked fine until we connected again and he told me how his life had completely fallen apart. He said, "I remember you told me that when the real world overtakes your made-up world, you're going to implode." That's what happened; he completely imploded. He said he considered taking his life several times. Moreover, he said that he could no longer suppress and compartmentalize his experience. I asked him why he didn't get help sooner. He said that as a man he thought he had to figure it out on his own. If you're honest with yourself, you've lived that belief. That statement is part of the toxicity of manhood. We as men have been taught that we must solve our problems on our own internally and be Superman at the same time. No one can live up to that standard. The sad reality was that the man did more damage to himself holding it in than he did in finally acknowledging and accepting the truth of his situation. He not only damaged himself, he damaged his friendships and opportunities. Delusion will cost you way more than you're willing to pay. **What are you pretending to not know??** There are far too many of us playing pretend about things that we know we ought not to. I know of a man who deluded himself into thinking that he wasn't hurt that his father wasn't in his life. Again, like the other man, he looked as if he was living his best life. Whenever the subject came up, he would always quip, "Look how good I turned out without my daddy," or, "My daddy not being in my life was the best thing that happened to me." When his umpteenth relationship ended, he found himself sitting in his emotions, and he finally sought help through therapy. The therapist helped him unpack the root of his broken relationships: his father. He realized how much anger he had towards his father. He first acknowledged that he was hurt by his father's absence. He then accepted the fact that he was damaged by his relationship, and as much as he resented his father, he in some ways was just like him. He said it was the acceptance that led to him making the necessary changes in his life.

Serenity

I mentioned Alcoholics Anonymous in the previous chapter for their success in helping their members lead sober lives because they integrate acknowledgment into their model. Another thing they do is add the element of acceptance. Part of the practice of AA is they often recite the Serenity Prayer, which states:

"God grant us the serenity to accept the things we cannot change, the courage to change the things we can, and the wisdom to know the difference."

The prayer is simple, yet it's loaded with profundity as to how we are to accept things and navigate through life. The short prayer highlights the ingredients needed for acceptance and for a better life. God, peace, courage, and wisdom. You're going to need ALL four things if you're going to navigate through acceptance. I consciously didn't want to make a book specifically about God, because I wanted to be more universal in my approach, but the truth is God is my source and my life. I'd be remiss to not mention the power of the Lord in my life, especially as it pertains to surthriving. I'm going to be honest, you need God. It will take something outside of you to get you to a place of acceptance. Many of us have been through some egregious events. I can name many horrible situations I know of that would make you cringe. But I will say in every single case each person mentioned how it was God that brought them to a place of acceptance. I pray that you will take heed of this. Next the prayer highlights serenity. Another word for serenity is peace. There isn't a quantifiable number to qualify how precious and powerful peace is. As it pertains to acceptance, it shows up as a byproduct of embracing the situation. After you accept a situation, peace becomes your underpinning or foundation for you to go to the next level. Peace provides clarity and calmness. I always say that clarity precedes a breakthrough. That is what acceptance does. It sets us up on the path towards breakthrough. We break through the negativity. We break through the delusion. We break through the toxic masculinity. I've stated to you numerous times in this book already that courage and bravery are a part of acknowledgment and acceptance. Really at the heart of the concept of surthriving is courage: Courage beyond just staying at a place of just getting by or surviving a thing, but really pushing past it and going beyond the coming threshold. To transform your life, to become your best self, to lead and live in your purpose, you will have to have courage to do so. Lastly, wisdom, which is called the principal thing. Wisdom is defined as AR

Bernard says is the ability to discern and the courage to choose good over evil. In the case of surthriving, evil is remaining as you are. Wisdom is a gift that keeps on giving. Think about it, when you touch a hot stove, you accept that it's painful to touch. Thus, you are wise enough to know not to do it again. Wisdom is a gift of foresight. I mentioned that I had to manage my expectations of potential clients. I now can almost discern who is serious and who is half-hearted. That's because I've become wise enough to know and I accept that I'll always have to deal with this in some form or another.

We as men all have an area where we need to exercise the Serenity Prayer that leads to acceptance. My hope is that the acceptance needed will put you on a path to new beginnings and breakthroughs. I believe that you have the capacity and bandwidth to find the courage and the maturity to just accept things as they are and not as you wish. I offer up to you that it's time to stop denying, deluding, and lying to yourself. You've been hurt and experienced pain unmeasurable, and that's okay. That doesn't make you weak or less of a man because you're allowing yourself to accept it and experience it. It makes you clear about your desire for a better life that will help improve your relationships with others and yourself.

Surthrival Mode 3
ARTICULATION

"I had to resign to myself, many years ago, that I'm not too articulate on how I feel about things. I do that through my music."

— David Bowie

I remember being all of fifteen years old and I recall it seemingly as if I were in a cheesy episode of "Saved by the Bell." I overheard some girl that I liked refer to me as a faggot. By that time, I was so used to hearing that word that I wasn't necessarily hurt by the word as much as by who had said it about me. I thought she was my friend. I remember the wind being knocked out of me, and the weight of the blow almost caused a nauseating reaction. I found a bench to sit on, and I just collapsed. What I felt was defeat. I couldn't win this war or battle. I didn't know what was wrong with me, and I literally was tired of trying to find it out. My spirit was slowly waning, I felt a cloak of coldness cover my body, and I almost surrendered to it. At that very moment, a friend of mine, Nikki, sat down and handed me a CD (I'm dating myself!), and said, "Go listen…" I went home and listened to the album, "My Life" by Mary J. Blige. It was the first time I was able to connect with an art form. The album articulated the anguish I was experiencing at the time. I didn't know the power of music and the arts until that moment. I didn't have the language nor lexicon needed to qualify and quantify the pain. My emotional intelligence was quite low. Why was that? Well I didn't see it modeled from either of my parents. As loving as they were, they were also very traditional, in a cultural sense. You didn't show emotion or talk about your feelings. You either sucked it up or you were deemed to be weak. Moreover, the hyper-masculine south dictates that feelings are for women and not men. I was suffering and screaming at a frequency that only I could hear. How was I to navigate through this?

What the album "My Life" provided for me was the ability to express and articulate with specificity the things I was experiencing. On the album Mary has a song "Be Happy." The chorus goes "All I really want, is to be happy. To find a love that's mine it would be so sweet." Those words are so simple yet so profound at the same time. I wanted to be happy. I wanted to love myself. I wanted to like myself. I wanted to be loved. I wanted to be healed of the trauma. However, the challenge was that I didn't have the words to say it. I didn't know how to say it. I didn't know why it was important to say it.

In my work with young men or even in my conversations with my male friends, I've found that many of us don't understand why articulating is important. "I feel a ways," is a statement I've heard so many young men or even grown men say. Now I want to make a distinction between acknowledgment and articulations. They are similar but extremely different, yet equally important. While it's important to acknowledge that one feels something, usually negative or traumatizing verbally or mentally, it's imperative that we first accept and then articulate what we're feeling and what that feeling is doing to us at the time. This is the part where most men check out mentally and emotionally.

Acknowledgment: Yes I've been hurt and I'm sure it has to do with my father's absence.

Acceptance: My father not being in my life has hurt me. I didn't ask for it, but I'm responsible for how my life is to go forth.

Articulation: My father's absence in my life has left

me feeling abandoned, broken, and inadequate. It has affected my life in many ways. I have trust issues and relationship issues as a result of this.

I could write more, but my point is to get you to understand the difference between acknowledgment, acceptance, and articulation and how they all work together. All three are necessary and required for Surthrival Mode to take place. A truth and principle I've discovered is that specificity sets the atmosphere for miracles and healing. So men, when we say I feel a ways or whatever variation of protected indifference we may express, we limit our ability to experience the miraculous and healing. Here's something else to think about: who can help you with a statement like "I feel a ways?" No one knows what that means! Now let's unpack this. Let's start with the positive. At least saying that you feel something is in itself positive. So there is acknowledgment taking place. However, it ends there. What are you feeling and what has it done to you? This is where having an emotional lexicon comes into place. At the heart of emotional intelligence is being able to articulate the emotion one is experiencing and being able to navigate through it. The reason why many of us men are stuck in life in many areas is because we don't know the emotions we're experiencing let alone know how to navigate through them.

Here's a reality: help can come to a person that says, *Hey I'm feeling really hurt or saddened by the incident.* Why? Because the person identified what the emotion was and what caused the emotion to happen. Ideally, the next step is to express what the emotion has done and how it has affected your life. This is important because it provides a framework for help. When we limit our language, we limit our healing. It's just that simple.

For many of us men, we have low EQ's for a lot of reasons. The culture is obviously one. The fact that we have never seen it demonstrated in our lives is another. But one more reason that may be overlooked is the fact that on average men speak 10,000 words a day and women speak at least 30,000 words a day. That doesn't mean that all men don't know how to identify emotions. It typically means that we'll go for the shortest, succinct verbiage to explain our feelings. The danger again is it limits our human experience, and it limits our ability to be understood. What I'm offering is that we as men need to begin expanding our words just a tad bit more. Emotions have different varying degrees of intensity, depth, and range. So an emotion like the word *mad* sits on a spectrum that includes: perturbed, fury, rage, contempt, pissed off, anger, and livid. There are more that I can name. The point is this: while all the emotions above are similar, the degree and intensity in which they are experienced is different. You don't handle a person who's mad the same way you handle a person who's enraged. The same is true with other emotions. For example, with sadness we have other emotions like: somberness, regret, dejectedness, gloom, grief, sorrow, and depression. We don't handle them the same. In order for us to heal, we have to know what it is we're experiencing. Understanding and articulating our experiences helps create a better relationship, not only with ourselves and others, but it also helps us with our relationship to the world.

For the most part, I've discovered that human beings are comfortable residing in two emotions: anger and indifference. Some may add frustration to the fray as well. For this book, we'll use anger and indifference. Here's the thing. Usually bubbling underneath anger and indifference is hurt. What's underneath the hurt is disappointment. Underneath the disappointment is an expectation not met. A lot of hurt we experience, no matter our gender, is based upon an unmet expectation. Usually that expectation is not articulated. Now to be fair, we as kids didn't necessarily know how to articulate our expectations of our parents or other relationships. However, we should be able to articulate what our expectations are as adults.

The example I used earlier of the staff development training I did in Washington, D.C. punctuates the importance of this. Every man at the training shared and expressed his deepest pains. One young man was courageous enough to share about his anger towards his family, especially his mother, father, and grandmother, for being addicted to crack. He shared that before the training he found his grandmother in a crack-induced coma. He also added that there was no food in the refrigerator. He was so angry that as he spoke, the anger slowly transitioned into hurt and he began to sob. He cried for what seemed like an eternity. He was able to say what the hurt had done to him. He didn't want to feel anything. He was embarrassed, and he admitted that most of his behavior problems stemmed from being so hurt by his family. I along with the counseling staff at the organization were able to help him and get him on a road towards the healing and freedom he needed.

Sometimes articulation isn't always verbal. Sometimes what speaks the loudest isn't always words. The tears the young man cried accentuated the pain and turmoil he was going through. The sobbing articulated that he'd been holding in his shame and anguish for many years. Additionally, the tears articulated that the dam of his emotions could no longer withstand another moment of denial. I can relate to that experience. My tears have many times articulated what I couldn't express verbally. I remember when my father passed. I remember it so vividly. I was watching the movie "The Forgotten" and I got a phone call from my mother that my father was in the hospital for cardiac arrest. At the time I didn't know that sometimes cardiac arrest is related to drug usage.

Fast-forward, suddenly I'm on a plane back to Dallas and I have to help my mom plan a funeral. In my heart I knew that I needed to cry over my daddy, but I truly thought that I was doing the right thing by not expressing my feelings. Seeing him in the casket made me almost faint, but I had to suck it up and be strong. I was so adamant about sticking to my guns that at the wake I told my brother and sister not to cry. What the hell was I thinking? At the funeral I went so far as to say that I didn't want a scene or any emotional outbursts of any kind. I was very serious about it. I told my aunts and grandmother, his sisters, and mother not to cry. I guess looking back I was somehow making up for all the times I was made fun of for being too emotional or sensitive. After the funeral I found myself back in New York. I was depressed, but I was doing my best to hide it. One day on the train, I was listening to music and I saw someone who looked like my dad. I literally had a breakdown on the subway. Everyone in the car looked at me and I just fell to the ground and sobbed. I missed my daddy. My tears and sobs articulated the abandonment I felt from my daddy and embarrassment over how he died. Moreover, my emotions screamed the loss of my biggest inspiration. This brief story just highlights the fact that sometimes our emotions can provide a richer context of our experience more than our words can.

However, we can never negate the power of words. I've learned in my brief journey that words are spirits. They create worlds, universes, and perceptions. They are the foundation of life. Words truly capture the human experience. The biggest lie ever told was, "Words don't hurt." If we're honest with ourselves we know that statement isn't true. We've all been hurt by words. Words have taken people over the edge. Words have caused folks to cave in and stop living. Words have caused us to believe we aren't worth anything. Words have shaped our very lives. The bullying I experienced caused me to articulate a longing for it to stop and to find peace. However, what I was articulating was the notion of knowing what I didn't want.

When you ask people what they want, you're asking them to specifically speak life to their innermost desires. I've come to discover that people know what they want deep inside. The problem is that folks don't have the language to express the need or desire. If we can barely articulate what we want, how much are we able to articulate the pain and adversity we've experienced?

It's hard to tell your story without somehow feeling like in some way it's your fault. As humans, I think we tend to take on what doesn't belong to us, and what does belong to us we leave behind. Life is funny that way. At the core of it, we often feel like we could have done things differently. I know with the bullying I experienced, I used to find myself getting extremely angry because I was afraid to stand up for myself. The truth is, at the moment that was my truth. I was scared and afraid to defend myself. Thankfully, today I can now look back at my life with a positive resolve. However, there are many of us who can't. What I've come to discover is that when we can't articulate or express our pain, the pain remains in control of our lives. We become its subjects. So men, I'm offering this up to you: you can usurp the pain's authority in your life by simply speaking about it. This is so simple yet so hard for most of us. We tend to protect ourselves even more when trauma happens.

It's the "how" that leaves many of us tripped up. As with a lot of things in life, it's about perspective. Taking on a massive undertaking like sharing our emotions or pain is a very large mountain to conquer. Especially if we are accustomed to maneuvering through life differently. The best advice is to take things in parts. Piece by piece. So for instance, if you are articulating your needs, emotions, or experiences, first begin by sharing what you feel comfortable in sharing. Here's the caveat: it has to be something out of your comfort zone—meaning, use different language to capture the moment. For example, instead of saying, "That situation has me tight," try saying, "I had an experience that really left me feeling upset and I almost lost it for a second." In the first statement all you did was just acknowledge the situation. With the second statement, however, you acknowledged, accepted, and articulated the experience. All that changed was the language used.

To add to this, I want to stress the importance of using your discernment and discretion with what and with whom you share or articulate your truth.

I believe that because we live in a time of social media and catfishing we fall into two categories: too trusting and not trusting at all. We have to strike a balance, and the only way to do so is to use discernment. Discernment is being able to perceive, distinguish, and judge a thing well. This is important because not everyone will have your best interest at heart. This can include family, friends, co-workers, etc. Everybody doesn't need to know all of your business. But, we must be able to identify those who have proven themselves to be consistent, honest, and trustworthy. These are the attributes to look for in a person. Even in romantic relationships, we must also exercise discernment. I've experienced harsh judgement from an ex-girlfriend when I expressed that I had been molested. At first she seemed cool with it, but when we would get into disagreements she would bring it back up. I felt betrayed. I felt as though she took my delicate heart and smashed it into pieces with her sledgehammer of a tongue. I never shared or articulated much of anything with her after that violation. I thought I was alone in my experience. I came to find out either through my coaching clients or just talks with friends that they experienced this too. The truth is that as men we are very fragile with our hearts and its contents. Once there's been an infraction, it's almost impossible to get back inside. Even with the potential danger of articulating, the good of it still outweighs the bad. There is power in declaring and sharing. Remember the power of a secret is in keeping it and not the secret itself.

I do feel it would be remiss of me to not insert the need and vital importance of therapy. Therapy is great because its only objective is to see you well. Seeing a therapist consistently over time helps you to find comfort in expression and articulating. Therapists are trained in various approaches to help you unpack, find the pathology of a thing, and process. They are completely unbiased and objective (well, they should be). Moreover, they are to create a safe space and environment for you to feel secure. Now realistically speaking, I know there's a stigma attached to men and therapy. There's an even bigger stigma attached to black men and therapy. I for one am a proud black man who has benefitted extremely from therapy. I've also encouraged several male friends of mine to see a therapist, and they've experienced great results. This book isn't a public service announcement for you to go to therapy. I feel it's my job and responsibility to let you know of the great benefits of therapy and to let you know it's okay if you see a therapist. You're not broken; you just have some things that aren't working. It's really about reorienting our minds about all of this stuff. A man takes responsibility for his life and the healing of his life. Therapy is a great way to do so.

Now I also understand that for many of you, you won't go see a therapist (just yet) and this book may be the closest thing you'll get to therapy. That's also why I want to provide you with as much rich content as I can. I want to provide you with tools that you're going to need if you wish to thrive in life.

Circling back to tips on articulating, we covered taking things in pieces and using language outside of our comfort zones. With language specifically, there are certain techniques we can start to use.

Sensory language is a powerful tool in appealing to all five senses to provide a richer more in-depth context for the articulating. There's a science to sensory language. It provides a deeper more intimate connection between the narrator and the audience. So using words that heighten the senses makes for a deeper connection and helps us to improve as communicators. Sensory language also heightens our abilities to be understood fully. One of the greatest pains in life is being misunderstood. I know as men we feel that way because we are often so insular with our emotions and issues that when we attempt to express them, we fail to truly express our truths. Moreover, we can tend to feel worse than before because we know (1) that we didn't communicate thoroughly enough and (2) we know the person we're speaking to didn't grasp it the way we hoped. Using sensory language is a great remedy to that problem. Here's an example of using sensory language versus regular language:

RL: Today I had a really bad day.
SL: Today was percolating with negativity. At every corner I seemed to smash into nonsense.

The first example does provide the context; however, it's very short and succinct. But in order to open ourselves to becoming better communicators and expanding our bandwidth as men, we need to learn how to articulate our experiences with specificity. Be honest, yes you may have had a bad day, but it possibly could have triggered some old feelings, thoughts, or experiences that you don't want to revisit and potentially sent you spiraling into a pit of despair.

Would you be content with just saying you had a bad day knowing that there's so many layers to this onion? Sensory language creates intimacy. Sensory language helps you to exert your power over the situation because you control the words to describe the situation.

Another great tip for articulating is to use technology. I use this technique with a lot of my male clients. Have you ever watched a reality TV show and you see the characters talking to the camera? Well that's called a confessional. I like to create confessionals with my clients. I've understood throughout life that people like to vent when no one is around. I know I can't be the only one??? I'm willing to bet that I'm not. Creating your own personal confessional is an excellent way of allowing yourself the permission to share without judgment your deepest thoughts and issues. Also another benefit is that it helps you to form language. If you make it a practice, it allows you space to begin to formulate an incorporate sensory language, taking things in pieces. The greatest thing about this technique is that it can be done almost anytime anywhere. Now I recommend you do this in your own privacy. You can use your phone. I like to use my computer and use the Photo Booth app for Mac. I'm certain that if I ever lose my computer that whoever finds it will be in for a show. I have tons of confessional videos. They have helped me to contextualize my experience, which in turn has helped me to process my experiences, which led to me being healed of certain situations.

Going to graduate school provided many benefits that I'm extremely grateful for. I mean who doesn't like saying I went to Columbia University for my master's in Psychology? It just has a nice ring to it. All jokes aside, the rich experience exceeded the academics. The director of my program, Dr. Lisa Miller, hit the nail on the head when she said that the best thing that higher education provides you is a lexicon. Language as I've stated numerous times is the most important thing when it comes to articulation. Dr. A.R. Bernard says that, "He who controls the language controls the conversation." When I'm working with young men via my program Alchemic Solutions, one of the first things my partner Jeff and I do is introduce the students to a new vocabulary word for the session. For example, we used the word *transmute*. Transmute means change in form, nature, or substance. We incorporate the term all throughout the lesson and use inculcation (repetition) to ingrain the word into the minds of our young men. We then build upon the word with a new word the following session. What does this have to do with you?

I want you to find a new word to incorporate into your daily lexicon. As emphasized earlier, with incorporating new language, the distinction with this is I want you to research a new term on your own. For instance, research a new word that you would like to transmute and integrate into your daily language. Again, the purpose is to expand your bandwidth as a man, as a human.

So let's review the tips for articulation:

1. Take things piece by piece.
2. Try your best to not use familiar phrasing.
3. Use sensory language.
4. Video Confessional.
5. Research, discover, and apply a new word to your lexicon.

These are practical steps that you can start implementing and exercising. These tips along with the overall modes of surthriving require consistency and intentionality. So you must do these things on purpose and for a purpose if you are to see the results you desire.

Surthrival Mode 4
ALCHEMY

"We are master alchemists: we may not have discovered how to make gold out of lead, but we are able to make heaven out of hell..."

— *Khang Kijarro Nguyen*

When most people hear the word *alchemy* they think of the book "The Alchemist" by Paulo Coelho. It's a book about the process and the journey of life. It highlights that if we persist we too can find the magical treasure that's inside of us. The book does focus on the art of alchemy, which is transforming one thing to another thing that is of greater value. This is usually in reference to turning lead into gold. I'm not being New Age by any means. But, I do like and love the concept of transforming one thing to another (and that thing being of greater value than it was before).

That's why my business partner Jeff and I decided to call our program for young men Alchemic Solutions, which I mentioned before. At the core of it, we believe that young men of color are 21st century alchemists who are able to transmute the narrative of what it means to be young, black, male, and gifted. We believe that they have within them currently all they need to become who they desire to be. Moreover, they are the agents of change and the authors of the narrative they choose to write. What is true for them, our young men, is true for us grown men. This is the fourth and final A of surthriving. Whatever it is we've experienced in our lives, we have the ability to overcome it and turn it into something of greater value. Everyone has alchemic power within them. Tapping into our alchemic powers is the stage where we go from victimization to victor.

As I've shared throughout the book, I've experienced a lot of pain. The emasculation I experienced growing up left me in a suicidal state. It wasn't just peers who made fun of me. It was also family and members of the church. I felt that I didn't matter. I felt that I had nothing to offer this world. I felt inadequate and incapable of just being. *Through prayer, therapy, and actively engaging acknowledgment, acceptance, articulation, and alchemy I now stand today as a man who was once crushed in his masculinity to a man who empowers men in their masculinity.* I took what was deemed worthless and I turned my narrative into something of greater value than it was before.

I think about Jesus. He was the ultimate alchemist. I don't find it to be a coincidence that the first miracle he performed that was documented was turning water into wine. Its symbolism is profound, and theology has been developed from it. But the literal interpretation for me is that something ordinary can be turned into something extraordinary. We all start out as water. When life happens and we get hurt and we experience hardship, abuse, rejections, and hell, the water gets murky. I've listed in this book several individuals (I purposely chose men) who have turned their murky waters into savory sweet wines.

In my work with young men as well as adult clients I do an exercise called Then and Now. I show pictures of notable male figures from all realms of influence. I show a picture of who they used to be and who they are today. Next, I create two columns labeled Then and Now (I make sure to create a space between the two columns). I ask them to list the attributes or characteristics of the Then picture. Then I go to the Now column and repeat the same steps. Now here's the powerful part. I referenced creating a gap between the columns. This chasm between the two is where the alchemy takes place. I ask my clients, "What do you think happened between the Then and Now?" This is where we engage in critical thinking. What are the possibilities that could have taken place? What do you think the person got curious about? These are the type of questions I have them reflect upon.

Gentlemen, I'm proposing that if you're reading this book that you are in your Then. The Then is composed of your current way of handling your emotions, pains, traumas, limited vocabulary, and relationships. Your Now space is truly up to you and your most vivid creative imagination. You have the tools if you apply them, to shape and craft a beautiful now. What are you willing to get curious about? Here are some questions to get you started:

- Since nothing's wasted in my life, how can I use all that I've experienced to benefit others?
- What if I decided to address my emotions head on?
- The next time I feel overwhelmed in my thoughts and emotions, what am I going to do that's good for me?
- What would happen if I started to really articulate my experiences? How might it benefit my relationships with others and myself?
- What if I showed my son that it's okay to cry and

experience emotions and that it's healthy in order to be healed?
- How would that affect his views on masculinity?
- What does a healed me look like?

Imagine your most ideal Now and begin to envision what that looks like. The space in between, the alchemy, is where the rubber meets the road. I'm sure you're asking yourself again, *How?* So there are a few ways to begin to actually engage in the transformation and finally reach the stage of surthrival. The biggest thing to know is that this is a process. We hear it all the time, but we truly need to understand this. We understand it in theory, but living it out is totally different. So many of us freak out when things don't materialize as quickly as possible. My friends that are health coaches and fitness trainers tell me all the time about their clients who start a new diet or weight training program. They say that clients will be on a diet or workout routine for a week and expect to have a six pack and be instantly healthier. While we all would love that to be the reality, it's just not. So men, you have to resolve within your soul that all of the contents of this book is a process that will have an expected end. The end is not the focus; it's the transformation of who you become and the story that takes place that should be the focal point. We have been having it all wrong. We as men are results-oriented. We look at output and expect a reasonable outcome.

The power lies in the story of it all. Think about it: it's testimonials that are more than likely to take you over the hump to purchasing something or a service. Why? We all love a story. A story activates our ability to wonder, envision, and dream, and it connects us to possibilities. Stories are so powerful that organizations and coaches are paid handsomely to help CEOs and notable figures craft stories to connect with their staff and potential investors.

I shared in the beginning that I always provide my story whenever I'm in front of a group of people. I think it's important that folks know I had a "then" and they're witnessing my "now." I conveyed my story in parts in this book, for the sole purpose of connecting with you. I know that we may not meet face to face, but I wanted my soul to be felt in these pages. I'm so for you surthriving over your emotions and pain that I wanted to share things I'd never talked about publicly before. The story isn't just for you, it's for someone else. The story is the evidence that surthriving is possible.

Earlier in the book, I stated that most men are

comfortable in two emotions: anger or indifference, which is a numbness (so no feeling at all). What I'm proposing next as a step of alchemy is sitting in the pain and harshness of your trauma. I know that may sound counterproductive, but our tendency is to run away from the pain. I recall when Jay-Z said in a song, *"Can't run from the pain, go towards it."* He's absolutely right. In the pain, in the hurt, that's where the healing begins. Like the gentleman I mentioned who cried over the death of his mother, the ability to sit in the hurt and longing for his mother was the onset of his healing. Sitting in your mess is a powerful experience. Here's what most people miss: when you sit in your pain and let the emotions have their way (keep in mind we don't make decisions based on what we're feeling for the feelings will pass, we must make decisions based on information, discernment, and reasoning), when those moments arise that trigger the pain, the pain becomes less and the intensity of it weakens. When I allowed myself to sit in the pain of the betrayal of a friend, whenever I would see him or a trigger happened, the feeling of betrayal weakened severely to the point that I now feel nothing towards the situation. That's because I allowed myself to process through the emotions and thoughts that supported the pain.

I've focused a ton on emotions for a specific reason. It's my belief that a great amount (not all) of the mental health issues we see in the world currently first began as an emotion not dealt with. *So in a lot of ways mental health is emotional health.* Another reason why experiencing and sitting in the emotion is a benefit is because it allows you to know your bandwidth as it pertains to self-control and the point of no return. This is super important for men to be able to harness this self-control and intelligence. As men, we tend to be ticking time bombs that any slight trigger can send us off the deep end. Additionally, this step allows us to decide. Here's the painful truth: though we may have (not all of us) low emotional intelligence, we still are responsible for our emotions and our decisions we choose to make with or without them. The goal of us as men is learning to respond— not react—to life and its curveballs. Responding is rooted in the positive while reacting is rooted in the negative. When you are allergic to something it's typically known as a reaction. Allergies as far as I know have never been positive (smile). When you are sick and the medical professionals give you antibiotics, they are looking for how you respond to the treatment.

I must admit this step in alchemy really was hard for me.

I had to do this with every single trauma I've had in my life. Though I may have thought some really crazy things and in the apex of the emotion as the volcano of emotions began to erupt, I sat in it and chose to not react. With all the fire and fury and the justification of wrong and trauma done to me, I learned to control my emotions instead of them controlling me.

Thoughts

If I were to ask you what is a recurring thought that runs through your mind daily, I'd be willing to bet that it's negative. Our thoughts are powerful. They sink down into the deepest parts of our being and when they've sunk deep enough, we begin to utter them. Our language becomes foul and negative. We then sink into abysmal dreariness. I've been there numerous times! I'm sure you have too. For me, it was a thought of inadequacy that looped liked clockwork in my brain 24/7. I had to cut the tape symbolically. I started to speak back to my thoughts. I understand that the brain is wired for negativity. Which is why it's easier for you to recall a negative experience rather than a positive one. So I had to fight my thoughts with positive thoughts and words. Even on those days when I could barely get out of bed, I found the strength to fight. I mentioned neuroplasticity in the first module of acknowledgment. That process is alchemy. We can alter our brains through the positive practice of challenging our thoughts with positive ones. I can't tell you how many times I've sent myself into spiraling depression over a thought. Oftentimes when I look back, the thought wasn't even legitimate. When I found myself engaging in positive thinking, I found my life was much better, even if my circumstances hadn't changed. But guess what? My circumstances did change. So my brothers, bathe yourself in positive words and thoughts.

Forgiveness

Everywhere you go you hear folks talking about forgiveness. The reason why this is an important, vital ingredient to alchemy as it relates to surthriving is because so many of us men are walking around bitter, mad, and lashing out at folks who didn't hurt us. I can tell you many things about forgiveness. The biggest takeaway that I can give you about forgiveness is that as long as you remain in an unforgiving state, that person is in control of that part of your life. You'll never own that part of yourself again until you do forgive that person. Imagine walking through life with literal holes on your body. People could see right through you. These holes represent the pieces of you that no longer belong to you because they are in the hands of the person who hurt you. That's a crazy picture right? Someone being in charge of your soul all because you won't forgive them and let go. Here's a painful reality: being unforgiving will hurt you more than the actual infraction done to you. What tends to happen is when we've been mistreated, we usually pick up where our abusers left off IF we don't forgive. So as much as it hurts, my brother, please find it within your heart to forgive them. You are worth so much more than the bitterness and holes in your heart. You deserve to be whole.

Persisting

As you envision your Now and are actively putting together all the elements discussed in this book, you make the decision to be relentless in your pursuit of transforming your narrative. Moreover, you seek it like gold to bridge the gap between surviving and thriving. Commit yourself to believing that no matter what happens, you're determined to see the transformation of your life take place. In a process of healing they call this persisting. To persist means to be tenacious, unmoved, and unwavering in your pursuits. In this stage of alchemy, my creativity got activated. I asked myself, *How can all this stuff I've been through be used? How can I continue to live and surthrive with all I've experienced?* As highlighted earlier, I got in tune with my story and I realized that if I experienced a wound to my masculinity then others must have too. In persisting I found my voice and power. In persisting I discovered that my pain can be a purpose and that purpose can turn into power, which can lead to a profit. As a coach, I've worked with celebrities, executives, organizations, and coached hundreds of men to greatness. Persisting teaches you that nothing is wasted in your journey. Nothing. All can be used. I've mentioned a few people who have learned to persist to the point of surthrival. What about you? Do you have what it takes? I not only think, but I know you do.

Self-Care

It would be remiss of me to not mention the importance of taking care of yourself in the midst of this ongoing process. We as men often use our self-care or coping mechanisms as reason to escape or dull ourselves from reality. In this instance I'm speaking of self-care as something that truly makes you feel good, alive, and is healthy for you. Whether it be exercising, eating better, vacationing, reading a book, resting, or just being kind to yourself, you must take care of yourself. I know many of us have responsibilities like families, careers, and tons of pressure from life. However, if you reference the tenets of this book, you know that we must be responsible and intentional in our mental and emotional health.

Accountability

We all need a sounding board and support system to grow in life. As Dr. A.R. Bernard says, "We don't grow in isolation, we grow only in the context of community." Imagine a plant. Yes, it may look like it's growing in isolation, but that's furthest from the truth. There is a community involved. It's a team effort! You have the seed, soil, water, sunlight, and air. All these elements working together create a plant. So fellas, the same is true for you and me. We need community that will hold us accountable. We need folk that will keep it real and 100 with us. I know this may not be easy, but it's doable. When I had an addiction to porn, I installed software that allowed my friends to monitor my activity. When I started the process of healing my emotions and mental health, I had somebody in place. On those nights when I felt like giving up and I didn't think I would make it, there were times when no one was available. Guess what? I had to learn how to (1) encourage myself and (2) learn to be my own accountability. I want a life of no excuses.

Conclusion

Gentlemen, if you've made it this far in the book, I just want to say I'm so proud of you. Yes you. We may never cross paths in real life, but you're in my heart and I'm rooting for you. The greatest movements or impacts in life all begin with a mustard seed of faith. I for the longest wanted to write a book for men, but I didn't feel qualified enough. Nor did I have the "language" to articulate what I wanted to say. It's my sincerest prayer that you get it. All of it. That you begin to break the cycles that have been embedded in our families, communities, and culture for so long. That we become countercultural and thusly create a new narrative. Furthermore, that we model for generations to come what it means to be a man, a healthy man who's responsible for his mental and emotional well-being.

As our society becomes more unglued from the Source, which I know to be God, we will see more and more breakdowns. Our threshold and tolerance for dysfunction has become weaker. We can no longer suppress or compartmentalize any more of our pains and traumas. The current mental health crisis is just that, a crisis. The only way to circumvent it is to truly confront it and do our best to conquer it. Remember, the mental and emotional imbalance is more often symptomatic. There is usually a deeper root cause attached to it. The imbalance serves as a warning. When our minds are in overload it will eventually pass on to the body. Everything is connected.

So as you walk across the bridge from surviving to thriving remember the process, the story, and how you are a true flesh-and-blood example of a man healed in his emotions and thoughts. It takes bravery and innovation to be something that never existed before. You have to get to a place where nothing is more important than your best life. I think of all the shame I felt attached to my life. I think about the anxiety I suffered through most of my twenties and how I NEVER want to experience that again. I had to shake off just getting by. I had to surthrive. I had to bridge the gap for me first. So I could help bridge the gap for others, including you.

You too will bridge the gap for others. I know it. I believe it. I feel it. So to close, I love you and can't wait to see how we collectively change the world by getting healed. As I say all the time, Be Great.

Your best is yet to come…